Hardy Garden Chrysanthemums

Judy Barker

HARDY PLANT SOCIETY

Gardening with hardy perennials

The first chrysanthemum popularised in English horticultural history was a very large, dark purple, loosely-incurving variety, descriptively named 'Old Purple'. This print is from *The Botanical Magazine, Volume 10* pages *327-329*, published February 1st, 1796 by William Curtis. When he wrote *"This Chrysanthemum appears to be a hardy greenhouse plant, and it is highly probably that, like the Camellia and Aucuba, it will bear the cold of our mild winters without injury,"* little could he have imagined more than two centuries later, over a hundred hardy cultivars would grace our gardens.

This series of booklets, produced by volunteers and published by the Hardy Plant Society, covers some of the most popular garden genera and some of the more unusual ones. Written by specialists in their field, each booklet contains cultivation and propagation advice with a descriptive list of good garden-worthy varieties. Booklets may be ordered direct from the HPS Administrator; details of which are found at www.hardy-plant.org.uk or ordered online.

Front cover: *Chrysanthemum* 'Cousin Joan' by John McCormack
Author: Judy Barker
Editor: Irene Tibbenham
Design & typesetting by: Goyle Weir, goyle@mac.com
Printed by:
TUDDENHAM PRESS
Design, Digital & Litho Printing
©**Hardy Plant Society October 2018**
ISBN: 13 978-0-901687-30-2

Gardening with hardy perennials

Hardy Plant Society

Formed in 1957 by a group of eminent gardeners and nurserymen, this international society has a large UK and overseas membership. It provides members with information about familiar and less-well-known perennials, and their cultivation. Through conservation and publicity, the Society works towards ensuring that many garden-worthy perennial plants remain in cultivation and have the widest possible distribution.

The Hardy Plant Society welcomes new members to join; please telephone the administrator on 01386 710 317 for details; or apply online at www.hardy-plant.org.uk.

The charitable objectives of the Society are:

- To advance the culture, study and improvement of hardy herbaceous plants
- To preserve the older, rare and lesser known hardy plants, cultivars and varieties from being forgotten and lost to cultivation
- To advance the knowledge of and foster public interest in hardy plants by the publication of information, by exhibitions or displays, by stimulating research and experiment and by awarding bursaries open to public competition
- To provide expositions of hardy plants at horticultural gardens and/or gardens open to the public, and to provide facilities for giving advice on the culture of hardy plants,
- To organise visits to places of interest in connection with the study of hardy plants and to co-operate with other bodies having similar or sympathetic aims
- To such acts as shall further the active and corporate life of the Society and which may lawfully be done by a public body established only for purposes recognized by the laws of the United Kingdom as charitable

Some of these objects are achieved through the publication of booklets such as this one on Hardy Garden Chrysanthemums.

www.hardy-plant.org.uk

Registered Charity No 208080

CONTENTS

Acknowledgements

Judy Barker
Around the year 2000 I started a journey collecting and studying hardy chrysanthemums, to find out why they are hardy when others sold as garden chrysanthemums fail miserably. Learning from Beth and Andrew Chatto's research on plant ecology and communities, I researched and liaised with people and institutions around the world to find out why some chrysanthemums are hardy and others are not. Please join me on this fascinating journey to help educate and popularise this hardy garden plant. The directory is full of tried and tested varieties recommended by myself and professional nursery growers.

Judy Barker, holder of a Plant Heritage National Plant Collection®, hardy chrysanthemum, was awarded the Chris Brickell award in July 2016 by Plant Heritage.

Dr Barrie Machin
I am indebted to my mentor and friend, the late Dr Barrie Machin for all his advice and encouragement over the years. An expert on breeding chrysanthemums, which he grew since the age of eleven until his death more than 70 years later, he was awarded the RHS Gold Veitch Memorial Medal for his work on All Year Round (AYR) cut-flower chrysanthemums; he was a member of the RHS Chrysanthemum Committee for many years and authored a number of books on growing chrysanthemums.

Dr Andrew Ward
Andrew is owner of Norwell Nurseries and Gardens, Newark, and prompted my initial interest in garden hardy chrysanthemums. He has now joined me as co-holder of a dispersed collection of hardy chrysanthemum, alongside Gary Leaver, Head Gardener, Hill Close Gardens, Warwick.

Photograph Contributors – *see page 87 for credits*
Alison Cundy, Anna Omiotek-Tott, Andrew Ward, Bob Brown, Gary Leaver, HPS Conservation, HPS Image Library, Irene Tibbenham, John McCormack, John Metcalfe, Judith Baker, Judy Barker, Lawrence Smith, Marianne Majerus, Martin Hughes-Jones, Pat Cryer, Peter Darrell, Rosemary Mitchell, Sophie Leguil, W. Atlee Burpee Company

Thanks also go to Plant Heritage for accreditation of the National Collections®; the RHS Trials Office for running the hardiness trials and inviting me to join the Chrysanthemum Trials Committee; Wallace Farr and Andrew McDougall; Graham Rice; Erik Benôit; the National Chrysanthemum Society; John McCormack for photography in all weathers, Kris Collins for proofreading, and all the enthusiastic HPS and Plant Heritage members who sent me damp Jiffy bags of material to grow with a view to naming and enjoy. Last but not least, thanks go to my husband Kenneth for his unstinting support and encouragement.

Introduction

To many people the name 'chrysanthemum' is more familiar as a cut flower, of which there exist thousands of cultivars, with new releases annually. Known variously as 'florists' chrysanthemums, 'pot mums' or 'exhibition' types, they are grown and shown by expert amateur and professional growers; but sadly most are disposed of when flowering has finished.

Fewer people are aware of a section of chrysanthemums, classified as Section 21, suited to growing in the garden which behave as hardy, herbaceous perennials; reliably returning year after year. Flowering from mid-August to late autumn/early winter, they bring a welcome climax of colour to the outdoor garden. We call these 'garden' or 'border' chrysanthemums, (winter asters in Europe), and though smaller in stature than indoor types, they share all other attributes of flower type, flower colour, variety and beauty whilst responding heroically to the outdoor forces of nature, including frost, wind and water. It is this group of chrysanthemums this booklet aims to highlight and encourage you the gardener to grow.

Generally trouble-free, they provide welcome colour to the climax of the gardening calendar. As Graham Stuart Thomas OBE once wrote …

"The chrysanthemum has always been a valuable autumn flower, and as one goes through towns and villages in October and November one is struck by the beauty of garden after garden full of old stalwart varieties; varieties that one sees again and again, in every district, in the same plots every year, undivided, unstaked, and often not manured. These sturdy plants are just what we need today; they go on year after year and are full and hardy and perennial needing no annual lifting and propagation by cuttings the disadvantage of many modern varieties….Chrysanthemums bring such a fresh fragrance and such beauty of colour into our gardens and rooms that all good varieties are welcome …."

The directory in this booklet provides detailed information on those 'good varieties'. The words 'hardy', 'garden', and 'border' chrysanthemums are used interchangeably.

History

In 1753, Swedish botanist Karl Linnaeus translated 'chrysos' and 'anthemon' literally from the Greek, the word chrysanthemum, meaning 'gold flower' alluding to the yellow petal colour of the plant then in cultivation and depicted in earlier illustrations.

Chrysanthemums were first used in China for centuries as a flowering herb, with breeding recorded as far back as 500 BC. The Chinese social philosopher Confucius wrote in his 'Li-Ki' book of protocol, "Chrysanthemums show their yellow flowers". White and purple chrysanthemums are recorded a century later.

Originally the exclusive domain of the Chinese Emperor's gardens, (being one of the 'four gentlemen' alongside the plum blossom, orchid and bamboo), they are said to have travelled a century later to Japan via Korea. Both cultures celebrate the chrysanthemum in culture and art. The Chinese and Japanese went on to develop and favour different forms; the Chinese crisply incurved, and the Japanese more exotic shapes. The highlights are covered below.

The chrysanthemum found itself in Japan by the 7th century AD, possibly via Buddhist monks, where the development of the floral forms we know today made a great leap forward, later popularised by the Chrysanthemum Shows of 900 AD. The Japanese flag depicts a red chrysanthemum with central disc and sixteen petals.

Though they can be traced to the Dutch books of the 17th century, it wasn't until 1789 that they were here to stay in the UK, when French merchant Pierre Blancard, of Marseilles, imported three varieties, white, purple and violet, from China.

Significantly, 'Old Purple' alone survived the journey. This descriptively named carnation-sized, semi-double, dark purple form, with loosely incurving petals, took its place as the first large flowering chrysanthemum in English horticultural history, quickly becoming popular in UK gardens during the 1790s. Flowering in 1795 at the nursery of Mr. Colville of the King's Road Chelsea, it was featured in the now famous William Curtis' The Botanical Magazine (later known as Curtis' Botanical Magazine) – *see inside front cover*. However, 'Old Purple' was not hardy, requiring glasshouse protection to flower well into late autumn.

The extreme popularity of 'Old Purple' led other countrymen to import further varieties direct from China and the Far East. This included the Royal Horticultural Society's fourth plant collector, John Parks, who sailed to China in 1821, returning in May 1824 with many chrysanthemums. These and others were later exhibited in 1826 at the society's garden in Chiswick; said to be nearly 700 plants in pots.

Of note were the 'Chusan daisies' (resembling pompons) by plant hunter Robert Fortune also sent by the RHS, this time in 1845. The Chusan daisy was propagated by the RHS and sent out to members, including a Parisian chrysanthemum enthusiast, Monsieur Lebois.

A French churchyard on All Saints' Day

Initial breeding attempts were made by Lebois who attempted to develop types that would grow outdoors in time for All Saints' Day (1st November).

In the 1850's these slightly hardier forms with an extended flowering season were named 'Early Flowering' varieties. Over time French and English breeders produced a limited number of varieties which flowered outside before October. From the 1850's these early-flowering varieties travelled across the Atlantic, often via French sailors, to the ports of New England. By 1900 gardeners in northern Europe and the northern states of America had available a selection of chrysanthemum varieties that flowered in mid-September until frost arrived to kill them off. The Americans called these 'garden mums', the English the 'Queen of Autumn'.

Subsequently and despite a centuries-long history of growing chrysanthemums in the Far East, a total metamorphosis occurred via concerted breeding efforts in the West to produce a series of garden hardy chrysanthemum cultivars, many of which we still grow today. These came about in the 20th century when the less-hardy and 'greenhouse' or 'exhibition' chrysanthemums from both China and Japan were crossed with extremely cold-tolerant species we now know to be one of two subspecies; *Chrysanthemum zawadaskii* subsp. *latilobum* and *Chrysanthemum zawadaskii* subsp. *sibiricum*, survivors from around latitude 45°N across Eurasia — the southern most edge of the last ice age.

The following section is an overview of this breeding history, of what are known as 'hardy garden chrysanthemums', 'border chrysanthemums', or colloquially as 'garden xanths' or simply 'garden mums', as well as some of the names of the people involved, as indeed there were many more.

Breeding Hardy Chrysanthemums
A journey across the world

Without the breeding efforts of the following people, the humble Chinese chrysanthemum might never have been crossed with the hardy species resulting in the garden forms of today. Besides winter hardiness, 20th century breeding objectives have also focused on flower colour, size, flower-form, weather-resistance, foliage texture, flowering time, plant habit, heat tolerance. Fragrance, frost tolerance, length of flowering period, as well as height, have also been considerations. Today the genetic make-up for most chrysanthemums is extremely complex.

1894 saw the launch of what we know today as the National Chrysanthemum Society, previously the Borough of Hackney Chrysanthemum Society at Stoke Newington, London, which began recording all newly introduced varieties, later formalised to a register in 1955. Its focus has been the development of greenhouse and exhibition cut flower types; the hardy chrysanthemums were not given their own group until 2006. Classified as 'section 21' they were trialled by the RHS for decades, despite being overwintered under glass. The addition of hardy garden chrysanthemums to the National Register is ongoing. Though hybridisation occurred throughout the centuries, we shall begin with Karl Foerster.

1909 – Karl Foerster
In Europe perhaps the most notable name for breeding hardy chrysanthemums was Karl Foerster, son of a nurseryman. Karl developed a specific interest in cold-hardy perennials generally, and chrysanthemum cultivars of his such as 'Brennpunkt', 'Citronella' and 'Goldmarianne', named for his daughter, are still around today. Though we do not have access to his breeding records, physical characteristics shown by these plants lead me to believe that hardy *zawadaskii* genes are present.

His article on cold-hardy Japanese Chrysanthemums for dry gardens, published in 1909, spring-boarded a prominent career in European horticulture. Then came World War 1 (July 1914 – November 1918).

1929—32 - Alex Cummings and the original Korean cultivars
Over the pond following the Great Depression of 1926, Alex Cumming obtained Korean-collected seed from Harlan Kelsey of Highland Nursery in North Carolina, which he used in his chrysanthemum breeding programme of 1931 to produce cold-hardy mums. He called this species *C. coreanum* and subsequently named the raised crosses 'Korean chrysanthemums'. It is believed these seeds originated from the Arnold Arboretum, Massachusetts. The Flora of China states "*Chrysanthemum zawadaskii* played a significant role in the development of the frost-hardy 'Korean chrysanthemums.' In 1905 Professor J Jack, of the Arnold Arboretum, USA, collected specimens from Poukan-shan mountain near Seoul, Korea, the plants of which were grown at the arboretum. It was Cumming's son, Roderick, who stated the species should be called *C. zawadaskii*

subsp. *sibericum* in the 1919 Arnoldia article that identified the Professor Jack introduction, though this has now been brought back to *C. zawadskii*.

Alex Cumming, originally a Scottish immigrant settling in Connecticut, carried out an extensive breeding programme for winter hardiness - the result ... a plethora of flower forms in a wide variety of shades and colours flowering from July to December. The first six cultivars released in 1932 were 'Apollo' (red bronze), 'Diana' (rose), 'Ceres' (bronze and gold), 'Daphne' (lilac-pink), 'Mars' (wine-red), and 'Mercury' (salmon). The launch of these first plants attracted the notice of Ben Wells of Hardy Plant Nurseries, Merstham in Surrey, and Alan Bloom, later of Bressingham Gardens, both of whom imported from Cumming's Bristol Nursery, Connecticut and launching them at the same time.

Alex Cummings then wrote and released a book titled 'Hardy Chrysanthemums' in 1939, further popularising this group of plants. Difficult to believe now, but by the end of the 1930s, garden chrysanthemums at one time were the most popular herbaceous plants being grown in British Gardens.

In America in 1930, the Plant Patent Act came into being, making it possible to patent a new plant, unlike Britain and Europe where a system of Plant Breeder's Rights (PBR) and Plant Variety Rights (PVR) exist to protect a breeder's investment. Between 1945—46 some of Cumming's Bristol Nurseries chrysanthemums were patented. Cummings described one of his introductions 'Chrysanthemum plant.

689' filed in 1945 as ... '*Although a heat resistant variety it is also more winter-hardy and better adapted to over-wintering under varying conditions than any other chrysanthemum variety of which I know.*'

See American plant patent above of one of Alex Cumming's chrysanthemums

1927—32 – Amos Perry and the Rubellums

A parallel stride made in the breeding of truly British-hardy chrysanthemums occurred when Amos Perry, a nurseryman based in Enfield, acquired *C. zawadskii* from three different sources. He trialled these side by side with existing non-hardy varieties in 1929. As Perry was advertising the Japanese forms, it is likely these were used in his breeding. That autumn, seed was collected and sown the following spring.

Flowering a year later, two seedlings stood out as different and improved in form from the species-type. These were named 'Anna Hay' (shell-pink) and 'Clara Curtis' (pale pink). Seed gathered from these plants led to further colour developments including a dark red-pink named 'Elizabeth Cowell' as well as a variety of plant heights. These cultivars were named 'Perry's Rubellum Chrysanthemums' because Kew botanist Sealy had named one of the sports from *C. zawadaskii* as a new species *Chrysanthemum rubellum*.

Becoming quickly popular in the 1930s, *The Times Survey of Gardening* wrote '...

still newer and of great promise for the future are the new forms of Chrysanthemum rubellum. The Rubellums outshine even the various Korean strains, in hardiness, range of colour and freedom of growth. They seem to flower unchecked no matter how hard the autumn nip, and to grow them in a roadside garden is to invite an almost embarrassing degree of attention and enquiry from passers-by.' Like Cumming's 'Koreans', Perry's 'Rubellums' were similarly sweetly scented.

Amos Perry retired in 1945 having released 25 distinct 'Rubellums' a fraction of the hundreds of hardy plants he bred at his nursery, Mr Perry's Hardy Plant Farm. He died in 1953.

Perry's catalogue from 1949 showing the original Chrysanthemum 'Clara Curtis', C. 'Elizabeth Cowell', and C. 'Anna Hay'

No. 551

Phone:
Enfield 4207-8, Night Extension: Enfield 0669.
Telegrams:
Perry, Nurseryman, Enfield.

SPECIAL
SPRING OFFER

of a few Sterling

Alpines and
Perennials

for Present Planting

Chrysanthemum rubellum: Clara Curtis, Elizabeth Cowell, Anna Hay.

PERRY'S HARDY PLANT FARM, ENFIELD
MIDDLESEX, ENGLAND

Transatlantic similarities

Both Alex Cummings and Amos Perry were using different subspecies of the wild forms of *C. zawadskii* at similar times to produce the Koreans and Rubellums hence the names are trade names of the original breeders and by today's standards of nomenclature should not be used as cultivar names.

Post-war there have been multiple crossings between the Koreans and the Rubellums. In 1948, 70 cultivars of Rubellums and Koreans were trialled at Wisley (overwintered under glass) and inspected by a joint committee of the RHS and NCS who made recommendations for awards. Few of those cultivars are still in commerce today.

More recently at RHS trials in Wisley, it was observed Rubellums and Koreans are similar in their main characteristics, though the Rubellums from the European type species have a more spreading rootstock and slightly more pronounced scent; as well as being more sensitive to winter wet compared with the Asian-form cultivars.

1930's America - Mums from Minnesota

When Professor of botany and avid plant breeder Dr. Ezra Jacob Kraus retired from the University of Chicago, he focused on breeding both chrysanthemums and day lilies also in the late 1930's. Teaming up with another breeder, Dick Lehman in Faribault, he acted as the commercial outlet for cultivars. Selling nationally via retail and mail order, Lehman coined the phrase 'Mums from Minnesota™'. The annual outdoor autumn display they

began continues to this day, attended by many. The business sold to Faribault Growers in 1972 and still sells hardy chrysanthemums including the lovely *C.* 'Ruby Mound' RHS AGM 2005.

C. 'Ruby Mound'

Also at the University of Minnesota, the breeding programme continues to produce winter hardy chrysanthemums, many of which are patented. However, trials in the UK found the winter wet did not suit them. Minnesota has much colder winters and generally remains frozen throughout the season; whilst the UK winters tend to be more freeze/thaw and wetter.

1938 UK – Fred Simpson

Ex-poultry farmer Fred Simpson of Otley, North Yorkshire, raised the 'Otley Koreans' throughout the 1940's and 50's. Having purchased Cumming's Bristol Nursery Koreans, he referred to them as 'tall and straggly with a poor colour range, flowering too late for the north of England'. His forms were shorter and earlier; though not being bred for hardiness, only 'Lucy Simpson' survives today. In those days a trade name was not protected and could be used by many.

1940's America - Yoder Brothers Inc.

Based in Cleveland Ohio, Yoder became notable chrysanthemum breeders and propagators, though plants were raised for autumn hardiness, not the winter. By 2004 the garden chrysanthemum was said to be the number one herbaceous perennial in the USA, referring to these cushion-types.

While US breeding continued during World War 2, the UK saw a demise of many perennials as the 'Dig for Victory' campaign of vegetable growing turned amenity growing spaces such as herbaceous borders, cottage gardens, even whole parks and gardens, into much needed allotments to feed the nation with fresh vegetables. Chrysanthemum breeding in Britain came to a halt.

1950s UK - Mrs Olive Murrell

Later picking up the mantle, an Orpington, Kent-based nurserywoman, Olive Murrell submitted as new, 'Orpington Korean Hybrids' to the RHS trials, having received seeds from Dr Eyres of Cincinnatti to add new forms. 'Wedding Day' is an Orpington cultivar listed since 1943.

C. 'Wedding Day'

1960-70s – Laurence Neel

Murrell's son-in-law Laurence Neel took over the sale and exhibition of Koreans at all the RHS Autumn Shows. Closing in the 1980's the Koreans were transferred to Mr Samuel Denis O'Brien Baker of Home Meadow Nursery Ltd, who continued to exhibit and sell at the RHS shows.

1970-80s – Samuel Denis O'Brien Baker

Home Meadow Nursery, Suffolk finished with chrysanthemums in 2004 and their collection travelled via Ivan Dickings, of Notcutts, then Harveys Garden Plants ending up at National Trust property Wimpole Estate, Cambridgeshire. Regrettably only a tiny fraction of those now exist.

HARDY PLANT SOCIETY

Gardening with hardy perennials

Recovering from the effects of WW2, efforts were made by organisations such as the Hardy Plant Society, started in 1967, to rescue and re-introduce some of these soon-to-disappear hardy herbaceous varieties of perennial plant. The HPS 'Conservation Group' continue this work today. The generous HPS seed exchange provided a genetic resource for gardeners throughout the country, and is still going strong today.

Later, the National Council for the Conservation for Plants and Gardens (NCCPG) was set up in 1978 to encourage the propagation of cultivated plants within Britain – a living library of

Plant Heritage

CONSERVING THE DIVERSITY OF GARDEN PLANTS

in Warwickshire and Norwell Nurseries in Nottinghamshire.

Today

UK nurserymen, such as Bob Brown and Dr Andrew Ward continue to launch new introductions. Eugen Schleipfer, Germany, and Thierry Delabroye, France, are notable breeders in Europe.

Author's allotment

plants cared for by passionate and knowledgeable persons. Now known as Plant Heritage, they manage a plethora of 'plant collections' around the country. A representative historical collection of what were previously known as the 'Korean' and 'Rubellum' types, (now known to be trade names) and 'hardy spray', from the 1920's to the 1970's is kept by myself, the author, across two allotments in London Colney. Additionally we now have a dispersed collection at Hill Close Gardens

Judy Barker's National Collection in London Colney

Botany and Classification

What are garden chrysanthemums?

Following extensive field trials at RHS Garden Wisley, hardy chrysanthemums are regarded as plants which not only survive winter cold, but survive in the ground over winter (H4 hardiness group and below). Plants behave as a true herbaceous perennial plant, returning every year after dying back to a woody base and re-sprouting the following spring from underground shoots.

Throughout history, the chrysanthemum has been repeatedly reclassified and historically you may find it under *Dendranthema*. A dicotyledon member of the *family Asteraceae*, inflorescences consist of a capitulum (head) made up of tightly packed individual blooms. The outer flowers, known as ray florets, are typically different in shape from the inner flowers, known as the disc florets. Ray florets are what we gardeners know as the petals. In double flowers the number of disc florets is reduced, and in fully double flowers the disc florets have been replaced by ray florets.

Generally, the chromosome number is 2n = 54, but can range from 18 to 90, with polyploidy lending great genetic flexibility to their phenotypes. This also provides an explanation for the high degree of reversion amongst some cultivars.

Flower forms

Chrysanthemum flower forms have been classified by the National Chrysanthemum Society (NCS), as follows.

(a) Anemones
(b) Pompons
(c) Reflexed
(d) Singles
(e) Intermediates
(f) Spider, Quills, Spoons (single or double) and any other type

However not all these forms are represented within Section 21, which are the hardy garden chrysanthemums.

Anemone flower form - *C.* 'Colsterworth'

Pompon flower form - *C.* 'Jante Wells'

Quilled spoon flower form - C. 'Syllabub'

Single flower form - C. 'Mary Stoker'

Single (duplex) flower - C. 'Cottage Yellow'

Spider flower form - C. 'Lindie'

Double flower form - C. 'Emperor of China'

The NCS have classified petal colours as follows, however not all hardy chrysanthemums have been assessed for inclusion to the Register. These colours are:

W	White	DY	Dark Yellow
DP	Dark Pink	LB	Light Bronze
LR	Light Red	Pu	Purple
Cr	Cream	LP	Light Pink
LS	Light Salmon	B	Bronze
R	Red	DPu	Deep Purple
Y	Yellow	P	Pink
S	Salmon	DB	Dark Bronze
DS	Deep Salmon	G	Green
DR	Dark Red	OC	other colours
LY	Light Yellow		These can have a suffix of any of
LPu	Light Purple		the other colours eg OC/DR

Flowering times are divided by the NCS into early-flowering (before 1st October), October-flowering, and late-flowering, based on open ground culture without protection of any sort.

Leaf forms

'Apollo' leaf topside

'Apollo' leaf underside

'Emperor of China' leaf topside

'Emperor of China' leaf underside

'Jante Wells' leaf topside

'Jante Wells' leaf underside

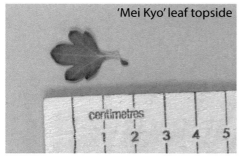

'Mei Kyo' leaf topside

'Mei Kyo' leaf underside

Leaves are generally grey-green, pinnatisect – but display huge variety between cultivars. They have a pungent and refreshing fragrance allied to lemon.

'Nancy Perry' leaf topside

'Nancy Perry' leaf underside

'Perry's Peach' leaf topside

'Perry's Peach' leaf underside

'Topsy' leaf topside

'Topsy' leaf underside

'Uri' leaf topside

'Uri' leaf underside

Hardiness

Chrysanthemum zawadaskii subsp. *latilobum* has been traced as the type-species that contributed cold hardiness and frost tolerance to the hardy cultivars we grow today; and can be found across Eurasia in different forms and subspecies.

Research reveals native habitats of species chrysanthemums include mountain slopes, sea shores, stream sides, and open grasslands. This indicates they are genetically resilient within a variety of habitats. Furthermore, these plants appear to grow in poor, sometimes calcicole, soils competing with other plants - perhaps there are alternative ecological or plant community relationships to be explored?

The true hardy border chrysanthemums are back crosses with the very hardy *C. zawadskii* and *C. morifolium* cultivars thereby concentrating the genes for winter survival outdoors. *C. zawadskii,*

Chrysanthemum zawadskii

occurs across the northern hemisphere at roughly 50°N from Europe to Asia. Nikolai Tzvelev in Flora of Russia (Komarov Botanical Institute) noted that this plant is a relatively old survivor, but fails to expound on 'relatively old to what'! This latitude is roughly at the southernmost edge of the last Ice Age, hence a possible explanation for the species ability to survive cold.

The first recorded European form was collected in July 1831 by Franz Herbich from the Pieniny Mountains W Carpathians and named in honour of Alexander Zawadzkii (1798-1868), a botanist and professor at the University of Lviv. A subsequent misspelling by Tzvelev changed the 'z' to an 's' in the name which now seems to be the accepted spelling.

Botanists have named many sub-species of *C. zawadskii* from Europe to Asia, but the one which seems to give not only winter cold tolerance but also UK winter wet tolerance is *C. zawadskii* subsp. *sibiricum* from Asia. When the European type is used in breeding then a free-draining soil is preferred, ie the plants behave as an alpine.

However, there are many other chrysanthemum species with a chromosome count starting from 2n=18 to 90. Though removed from chrysanthemum classification some have been used in past chrysanthemum breeding programmes. Breeding is mainly done using species with a chromosome count around the middle range 54.

Some cultivars can survive winter air temperatures as low as -50°C.

Illustration of *Chrysanthemum zawadskii* subsp. *latilobum* by Sue Ward

Life Cycle and Growth Stages

WINTER
EQUINOX

winter vernalisation
at least 4 weeks
cold below 4°C

Phase 3

Phase 1

Chrysanthemum
Life Cycle

**AUTUMN
EQUINOX**

flowering
phase

spring rhizomatous
roots send out new
shoots

**SPRING
EQUINOX**

vegetative
growth
phase **Phase 2**

budding up
summer plants respond
to temperature or long
nights trigger

SUMMER
EQUINOX

Chrysanthemums respond to stimuli in two ways depending on the type grown. A study of how different species respond would no doubt prove interesting. Some are short-day (or long-night) sensitive and others initiate buds in response to temperature, ie day neutral.

Chrysanthemums have three main phases:

Phase 1 dormancy occurs during the winter months when the plants have died down to below the ground level and formed rhizomatous roots. These rhizomatous roots are formed from subterranean stems and are charged with a food reserve. They sometimes travel a distance from the parent plant. The fine normal feeder roots die over winter. Each root possesses buds, nodes and scale-like leaves ready for the following spring.

Example of chrysanthemum rhizomatous roots.

Example of vegetative stage in chrysanthemum

Example of chrysanthemum cutting (unprepared)

Vernalisation below 4°C for 4–6 weeks is required to initiate buds for flowering even if overwintered in a greenhouse. Failure to achieve sufficiently cold temperatures for a sustained period results in continuance of the vegetative phase, ie a rosette of leaves that fail to lengthen or respond to growing stimuli. These will then produce either pale and premature stunted flowers if not abort flower formation completely.

Phase 2 starts in the spring as days lengthen and temperatures rise. New shoots emerge and the chrysanthemum steadily grows enough leaves on the stems to support subsequent flowering. Dr Machin observed that different cultivars of chrysanthemum require a set number of leaves to support flowering, so clearly something is counting!

This vegetative or juvenile phase lasts until mid-summer if not later depending on individual cultivar behaviour; allowing for cuttings to be taken throughout this phase.

They will readily root in 2–3 weeks if grown in gritty open compost in a protected frame. Removal of the soft top growth results in a bushier plant with increased side shoots, ie 'pinching out'.

Phase 3 is flowering, predominantly triggered by a chemical/hormonal switch at the apex of the shoot (meristem) activated by short-day length (long nights) when the plant has built up enough leaves to support reproduction. Some day-neutral cultivars flower when temperature is sufficiently high. The soft stems begin to stiffen and small green buds appear in the leaf axils, known as 'budding up'.

Example of chrysanthemum 'budding up'

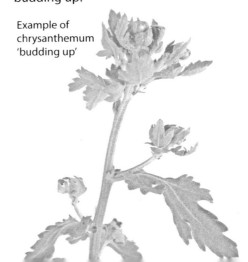

Cultivation

Hardy chrysanthemums are easy to grow as border perennials. They prefer a rich and loose, or well-drained soil that does not dry out in summer. Nevertheless, though hardy and easy to grow, they will thrive given extra care. They do well in a sunny border where the soil has been well prepared. A general fertiliser such as blood, fish, and bone or 'Growmore' worked into the soil each spring at a handful per square metre plus a good mulch of compost applied around the plants, will give them a good start to the season.

Plants do not require pinching and generally grow without support, though some cultivars will benefit from some staking, particularly if planted in an exposed or windy site.

I use Strulch®, a mineralised straw mulch, around the plant collection in late autumn, and again in the spring. This is a chopped wheat straw treated with an iron compound which deters slugs as well as providing cover over the soil preventing most weeds germinating, preventing water evaporation, soil capping and gradually breaking down contributing to the food source whilst adding to the soil structure. Another consideration, I find Strulch® is light and easy to apply but once down locks together preventing the wind blowing it all away.

This cultural advice applies to most other herbaceous perennials so the entire mixed border can be treated as a whole with maintenance. In spring keep a sharp eye for slug damage as the soil warms above 4°C, the main culprits being Keel slugs (*Tandonia budapestensis*) as opposed to the more noticeable surface slugs. Treat as necessary with slug bait, organic or otherwise.

Around the month of June, during the vegetative growth stage, the chrysanthemum plants, particularly after heavy rain, seem to need a boost and I find a light drench of liquid seaweed solution restores the leaves to a healthy green.

Check the plant growth carefully in spring as overcrowding leads to more problems than any other, so thin out any weaker shoots as you go around, if the plant's footprint is over 36cm in size do consider taking up and splitting in the spring or replace with new cuttings refreshing the soil around as you work.

In the garden border

Hardy chrysanthemums can be mixed with other herbaceous perennials. Varying in height from 45-150cm (if well fed), all flower forms are represented. Many are sweetly scented, providing a nectar feast late in the season for many insects.

As garden chrysanthemums are late-summer/autumn flowers, they are particularly useful inter-planted amongst borders with a bias to spring flowering, eg primroses, hellebores, *Dicentra*, *Viola* or spring bulbs which appreciate shade later. As these die down or fade after flowering, border chrysanthemums begin their rapid growth, providing cover for plants that fade untidily such as oriental poppies (*Papaver orientale* complex) and ornamental onions (*Allium* spp.)

Chrysanthemum border at Hill Close Gardens, Warwick

Chrysanthemum 'Rumplestilzchen' growing alongside an ornamental grass

Chrysanthemum border at Norwell Nurseries, Newark

Extend autumn interest with the use of asters, sedums, fuchsia, Japanese anemones and grasses.

Blending and contrasting of colour shades is a matter of personal choice – cultivars come in a huge range of colours. Mixing with plants of similar cultural needs will encourage stronger growth.

Tropical border from an Enfield garden, an example
of the flexibility of border chrysanthemums

Chrysanthemum 'Brennpunkt' growing alongside grasses at Bressingham Gardens, Norfolk

A mixed border planted up in the City of London, showcasing various foliage

Chrysanthemums provide late season nectar for butterflies such as red admiral (*Vanessa atalanta*)

Allelopathic interactions, whereby roots exude biochemicals that influence neighbouring plant growth, do occur with some cultivars. However, little published research exists to guide the gardener in deciding which plants should not be mixed with chrysanthemums in the border.

With careful planning it is possible to have wave after wave of fresh texture and colour from early summer to mid-November using hardy chrysanthemums.

After the show is over, cut down the stems by two thirds to reduce wind rock and any likelihood of disease build up by destroying these dead stems. Cover with another mulch to protect any roots just under the surface. A good indication as to hardiness is the amount of low basal growth visible at the base of the plant in autumn.

Beneficial Insects

As so many garden chrysanthemums flower later in the season, their scented nectar provides a welcome resource for insects and butterflies, particularly on a sunny, cold and windless autumn day.

Honeymooning hoverflies (*Helophilus pendulus*)

Chrysanthemum 'Cottage Apricot' and 'Cottage Lemon' share a vase

Recreation of a vase of mixed chrysanthemums from a 1960's Orpington catalogue front cover

Cut flowers

Though perhaps not as flamboyant as the greenhouse-grown cut flower varieties, garden chrysanthemums still make long lasting cut flowers and come in a variety of stem lengths.

Cut the stems close to the base of the plant, strip off the lower leaves, cut to required length of vase or arrangement, and plunge in fresh water.

Changing the water every 2–3 days will increase the longevity of the cut flowers.

Propagation

Hardy chrysanthemums have been known to grow for fifty plus years in country cottage gardens. Nevertheless, established plants can become leggy in the centre and reduce in vigour, so digging them up every 3–5 years to propagate and replant will help invigorate the clumps. Garden chrysanthemums are best propagated by division or cuttings in spring when the plants are in a vegetative growth phase until the summer equinox. Being short-day length (or long-night) sensitive, after this time bud initiation takes place, and rooting becomes difficult.

Division (basal cuttings)

In March or April when the weather allows, dig up a clump and divide into pieces, each with several shoots attached. They can be replanted directly in the ground, or planted up in pots, ideally in well-drained, loam-based compost. This is the fastest way to obtain strong, healthy plants.

Cuttings (softwood/stem)

These can be taken in late April, May and June. Water the plant and when turgid, choose a strong healthy shoot to snap off. Remove the lower leaves, 2–3cm; and place cuttings into a 50:50 mixture by volume of damp perlite (medium)/multi-purpose compost, and mist as appropriate. Roots should begin to form within two weeks. Pot up into separate

Softwood cutting (prepared)

pots, and label cultivar. Removing the top growth several weeks later will encourage lateral growth and a stronger plant for planting. Set out in a sunny position when plant looks sufficiently strong in May, or as local conditions dictate.

Seed

In the UK climate, chrysanthemums set seed when conditions are right, but these do not come true-to-type. They will however flower from seed the first year and may throw up some lovely surprises.

Should you be fortunate enough to obtain seed, or wish to pursue a breeding programme, seed should be sown in February–March, at a temperature of 10–13°C, and kept moist but not water-logged. Germination is usually quick.

Prick out seedlings into individual pots or plugs when large enough to handle.

Grow on, and plant out in May when plants have been hardened off, into their flowering position. A few can also be re-potted and grown under glass.

Chrysanthemum seedlings

Pests and Diseases

Having a mixed border will help to reduce the quantity of pests as a large stand of just one type of plant is more attractive to pests and encourages quicker multiplication. Within a mixed border planting there is a greater range of flowers offering nectar to beneficial insects, so a stable balance is easier to achieve. Good husbandry is another factor – particularly avoid overcrowding to facilitate air-flow through the plants. However, should your plants succumb to attack the following two are the most common.

Eelworm

Eelworms enter the root system via the ground water, presenting as leaf death starting at the base which rises progressively up the stem. The leaves also show brown triangle symptoms between the veins before dying completely.

Rust

There are two types of rust which affect chrysanthemums, namely brown rust (*Puccinia chrysanthemi*) and white rust (*Puccinia horiana*), both of which present as spots on the upper leaves with corresponding pustules on the underside. White rust is the more serious disease and quickly spreads and is difficult to control. A lot of chemicals have now been withdrawn and are unavailable to the general public and fungicides available from garden centres to use as a preventative will only give some protection. Also check the packet carefully as chrysanthemums are sensitive to some chemicals. With a very bad infestation spores can live not only in the plants but overwinter in the stools in which case dispose of heavily infected plants.

Treatment

If you have an affected plant and wish to keep it then the hot water treatment offers the best way for both white rust and eelworm infections. In autumn/late winter dig up the plant, cut down the top growth, carefully wash off all soil, (dispose of all the washings and top of the plant carefully), then immerse the roots in a bath of water at 45°C for 5 minutes; cool in cold water, drain well and pot up in fresh clean compost.

Other problems

Minor pests that may attack leaves and flowers include brown/black chrysanthemum aphids, leaf miners, thrips and earwigs, but in the garden, damage is mostly cosmetic.

As touched on previously, the use of slug bait will not go amiss. (Place slug pellets in a glass jar in the darkest, dampest part of your garden.)

A wet autumn may encourage fungal growth and moulds, in which case thin plants heavily and remove rotten foliage and flowers.

Viruses can infect plants on occasion, causing distortion and stunting of growing parts, but rarely kill.

TABLE OF WHITE RUST and WINTER WET SUSCEPTIBILITY OF SOME CULTIVARS

Cultivar	white rust		winter wet	
	resistant	less resistant	tolerant	not tolerant
Angelic	☺		☺☺	
Apollo	☺		☺☺	
Aunt Millicent		☹	☺☺	
Bronze Elegance	☺		☺☺	
Brown Eyes	☺			☹
Carmine Blush	☺		☺☺	
Cottage Apricot	☺		☺☺	
Cottage Yellow	☺		☺☺	
Cousin Joan	☺		☺☺	
Daniel Cooper	☺			☹
Dulwich Pink	☺			☹
Emperor of China	☺		☺☺	
Goldengreenheart	☺		☺☺	
Grandchild	☺			☹
Imp	☺			☹
Innocence	☺		☺☺	
Jante Wells	☺			☹
Leo	☺		☺	
Mary Stoker	☺			☹
Mei-Kyo	☺		☺☺	
Mrs Jessie Cooper	☺		☺☺	
Nantyderry Sunshine	☺		☺☺	
Perry's Peach	☺		☺☺	
Purleigh White	☺		☺☺	
Ruby Mound		☹		☹
Ruby Raynor		☹		☹
Spartan Canary		☹		☹
Starlet		☹		☹
Syllabub	☺			☹
Topsy	☺		☺☺	
Vagabond Prince	☺		☺☺	
White Tower	☺		☺☺	
Will's Wonderful	☺		☺☺	

Directory of Garden Hardy Chrysanthemums

The list of potential candidates for this directory is large, so the following cultivars are included based on National Plant Collection® holders' recommendations, and general availability for sale in Great Britain.

Since WW2 hundreds of hardy chrysanthemums have lost their names, passed around from garden to garden as they have been dropped from nursery lists. As a result, many have been 're-discovered' and re-named. Inadvertently this has led to some of the older cultivars being given new names. Equally many varieties have simply been lost in cultivation. Added to this, new seedlings and mutations have arisen. At the time of going to press, the names used in this booklet were considered valid. If you are able to share further background information on varieties covered in this directory, but not included here, please do contact the author.

The cultivars listed have a hardiness rating of H4 or below, unless listed otherwise, meaning plants are hardy outside throughout the British Isles in an average winter. Temperature -10 to -5°C (14 —23°F)

The chrysanthemum name is followed by:

- Other names under which it may be found
- RHS AGM with year of award: this chrysanthemum has been awarded the Royal Horticultural Society's Award of Garden Merit, meaning it performs well and will thrive in most garden conditions throughout the UK
- National Chrysanthemum Society Register – some outdoor hardy types have been classified as 'section 21' in the Chrysanthemum Register, but many more have the potential to be registered. Abbreviated next to the name as follows:
  Year of entry to Register
  Flower type: a=anemones, b=pompons, c=reflexed, d=singles, e=intermediates, f=spider, quills, spoons (single or double) and any other type.
  Colour abbreviations are as follows: W=white, DP=dark pink, LR=light red, Cr=cream, LS=light salmon, R=red, Y=yellow, S=salmon, DR=dark red, LY=light yellow, DS=deep salmon, LPu=light purple, DY=dark yellow, LB=light bronze, Pu=purple, LP=light pink, B=bronze, DPu=deep purple P=pink DB=dark bronze G=green OC=other colours which can have a suffix of any of the other colours eg OC/DR
  Example **'Agnes Ann'** 2006 21d DR added to registry in 2006, in section 21 with a single flower in deep red
- Height as grown in the national collections, which varies depending on soil, situation and temperature and is given as a guide only
- Flower description, size at maturity, colour, type etc which can vary according to differing environmental conditions
- Flowering time as a guideline, again variable as local conditions and annual weather patterns vary. Additionally, if street/garden night lighting is on overnight, flowering will be affected due to an insufficient night period.

- Foliage and habit information as available
- CWW – Care Winter Wet—meaning they can survive low temperatures, but are shallow rooters which means when heavy rain is followed by a freeze, the subsequent expansion of the ice tears the roots apart. Where they are growing on heavy soil, protection with a light loose mulch around plants in autumn, is recommended
- Breeding background and anecdotal information, as available

'**Acostie**'; ↕110cm; 6cm double bronze-red flowers; Oct–Nov; strong upright plant.

'Agnes Ann'

'Acostie'

'**Agnes Ann**'; 2006 21d DR; ↕46cm; 6cm double flowers in plum-red; Jul–Oct; and has weak stems. CWW

This cultivar is possibly an Otley Korean dated around 1940/1950s as stated in an old Collinwood catalogue and possibly bred by Fred Simpson who died in 1964.

'**Albert's yellow**'; 2006 21d Y; ↕76cm; 5cm single yellow flower, which takes on a red tinge as they fade, forming bunches at the end of the stems; Sep–Oct.

Raised by Mr Wright of Collinwood Nursery in the 1950s and named after his friend Mr Albert Butterworth.

'Albert's yellow'

'Alehmer Rote'; 2006 21d Pu; ↕80–105cm; 5cm bright pinky-red scented single flowers; Oct–Nov; the greyish finely-divided leaves form dome-shaped plants. CWW

'Alehmer Rote' habit

'Alehmer Rote'

'Aline'; 2006 21d LS; ↕90cm; 6cm duplex flowers of peach-flushed pink petals that are part quilled; late Aug–Sep, 'Aline' needs regular deadheading to keep it tidy. CWW
Listed in the 1980/81 Orpington catalogue and possibly raised by Laurence Neel.

'Aline'

'Alison'; 1973 29c OC; ↕120cm; single, pale-pink flowers, 7cm across with narrow petals; mid-Sep–Oct; a strong upright grower, very similar to Ann, Lady Brocket but grows with a very thick central trunk, forming good-sized clumps by the second year. CWW
Possibly raised by Jonas and Thomas Johnson of Tibshelf in the early 1970s.

'Alison'

'Alison's Dad'; ↕120cm; 7cm semi-double flowers in a lovely rich cerise-pink; Oct–Nov; foliage is a healthy green. CWW
This is a seedling grown by an HPS member's father, who passed it on to the collection.

'Alison's Dad'

'Anastasia'; 2006 21c DP; ↕60cm; 3cm petals shortening at the centre to give a flattened top to the deep mauve, magenta-pink pompon flowers; late Sep–Oct; it is susceptible to white rust. CWW

'Altgold'; ↕50cm; 1.5cm semi-pom flowers in a bronze-yellow; Oct–Nov; dome-shaped plants with small, dark-green leaves.
Raised and introduced by Karl Foerster in 1915.

'Anastasia' plant habit

'Altgold' early stage flowering

'Altgold' late stage flowering

Found in an 1882 Veitch nursery catalogue, Graham Stuart Thomas describes it in his book Perennial Garden Plants as *'A little "button variety" which is a sturdy plant and flowers freely every October and into November. Soft heather-pink.'* However, it has been reported in Foerster's 1920 catalogue leading to the suggestion it may even be an old German variety.

'Angela Blundell'

'Anne Ratsey'

'Angela Blundell'; ↕50cm; 3.5cm flowers with no eye but often with inky-black dots in the soft primrose-yellow centre; the small flowers age to white; Oct–Nov; the compact sprays makes a dense bush/ mound. CWW
Introduced by Bob Brown of Cotswold Garden Flowers.

'Angelic'; RHS AGM 2012; ↕70cm; 3cm across, white-flushed pink pompon flowers; late Sep–Nov; a weatherproof plant due to its upright self-supporting growth, it is a small-leaved bushy plant. CWW
The first mention of 'Angelic' is in a 1987 catalogue of Orpington Nurseries.

splashed with and lined in a rich pink. CWW
A sport of Nancy Perry, introduced by Sampford Shrubs in 2005, it was found and named by a Wellington (Somerset) gardener Simon Ratsey for his wife.

'Angelic' early flower | late flower

'Anne Ratsey'; ↕90cm; 5.5cm soft-yellow single flowers; late Sep–Nov; has a tendency to instability, for example whole plants recorded as reverting to pink; though these can vary from a lovely soft to a bright pink, with petals irregularly

reversion in 'Anne Ratsey'

'Apollo'

'Anne, Lady Brocket'; 2006 21d LP; ↕66cm; 8cm irridescent single pink flowers with paler salmon overtones and a yellow inner ring; Sep–Oct; stems are very lax and brittle. CWW
Raised by Amos Perry in 1940 and an original Rubellum trade name.

'Anne, Lady Brocket'

'Apollo'; 2006 21d B; ↕90–145cm; 4–5cm single, bronze-red duplex flower, flecked with yellow; the dark red buds give a pleasing contrast; uneven flower petals and a greenish centre; mid-Oct–Nov; 'Apollo' is a tough self-supporting, strong and upright growing plant that needs some space and makes an excellent bee-friendly border plant.
Bred by Alex Cumming 1940 and one of the original Bristol nursery Korean forms.

'Apollo'

'Aunt Millicent'

'Belle'

'Aunt Millicent'; RHS AGM 2009; 2006 21d LP; ↕75cm; the 6cm silvery-pink single flowers have a light yellow inner centre/ring; Sep–Oct; similar to 'Innocence' it forms pleasing dome-shaped plants covered with many starry flowers and needs a bit of elbow room to show herself at her best.

Found in an old garden in Kent by Mr Wright of Collinwood Nursery and named for the lady of the house.

'Beechcroft'; ↕90–115cm; 8–9cm pink-cream flowers are duplex but occasionally single, the darker buds give a beautiful two-tone effect as the flowers mature; Oct–Nov; an upright self-supporting plant with leaves that redden in autumn.

This is an old, tall and hardy cultivar bred by Halls of Heddon in the 1970s and named after Rosie Hardy's mother's house.

'Belle'; 2006 21d R; ↕80cm; the 5–6.5cm flowers are bright red to almost terracotta with 2–3 layers of uneven petals, intensifying as they mature; Aug–Sep; of upright sturdy growth, 'Belle' is a tough variety. CWW

Found in Home Meadow catalogues, 'Belle' may be an Oprington introduction, raised between 1960–1980.

'Beechcroft'

'Belle' flower spray

'Brennpunkt'

'Bretforton Road'

'Bretforton Road'; ↕65–85cm; 5–6cm cerise-pink duplex flowers; Oct–Nov; the brightly-coloured flowers are fantastic against the dark foliage, and plants form a pleasing shape making it a brilliant addition to the border. CWW

Introduced by Bob Brown of Badsey-based Cotswold Garden Flowers, who writes *"An interim name for a cultivar grown outside for generations in Badsey...."* after finding it in a garden there.

'Brennpunkt'; ↕80cm; 6–7cm double red flowers with a bronze reverse, fading to gold in the centre; Oct–Nov; this upright cultivar with dark red stems gives fantastic autumn colour and is great for cutting.

Raised in Germany by Karl Foerster, the name translates as 'focus/focal point' as in the focus of attention. See page 28.

'Breitner's Supreme'; ↕55–70cm; 4–6cm flowers are single, icy-white with a greenish centre; Oct–Nov; the dark-foliaged plants form a dome and the intense white flowers, called 'Dulux White' by a Norwell Nurseries customer can make it difficult to place in an autumn border, nevertheless when sensitively added, it makes a welcome show.

'Brennpunkt' habit

'Breitner's Supreme'

'Bright Eyes'

'Bright Eyes'; 1952 28 Y; ↕66cm; 3cm diameter, golden-yellow pompon flowers with a red centre; Sep–Oct; forms a low mound.
The origin is likely a Minnesota Mum, and it was listed in Roderick Cummings 1964 book.

'Bright Eyes' habit

'Brightness'

shaped plant covered in flowers which may be prolonged to at least three flushes with deadheading. CWW
Possibly raised by Fred Simpson of the Otley Koreans.

'Brightness'; 2006 21d R; ↕60cm; 4cm wide, bright-red semi-double and double flowers with a gold reverse and seven rows of petals; Aug–Sep; lovely neat-

'Brightness' habit

'Bronze Elegance' ('Peterkin', 'Bronze Mei-Kyo'); RHS AGM 2012; 2006 21dB; ↕50–85cm; 2–3cm bronze pompon flowers with small yellow centres flecked with reddish tones; Oct–Nov; very hardy with small leaves, the naturally branching plants form a dense spreading dome covered in flowers which sometimes revert to pink.
A sport of 'Mei-Kyo' occurring in 1971 and introduced by Ingwersen's Nursery.

'Bronze Elegance'

'Bronze Elite'; ↕90cm; 6cm single bronze duplex flowers; Sep–Oct; has dark glossy leaves and makes an upright plant suitable for cutting.
Raised by Elm House Nurseries as part of their Elite range which also included 'Pink Elite', 'Dark Elite' and 'Red Elite' and released in 1971 as part of their mail order range.

'Bronze Elite'

'Brown Eyes'

'Brown Eyes'; RHS AGM 2012; ↕40cm; 5cm sumptuously-coloured amber-bronze pompons with a small dark copper 'brown eye'; Sep–Oct; forms a low mound and can be used in pots, the small tightly-petalled flowers are weather-resistant making it useful as a cut flower. CWW
This 'Minnesota Mum' is also called 'button mum' due to its usefulness as a buttonhole and corsage, available for sale in the USA.

'Burnt Orange'; ↕140cm; 6cm quilled, burnt orange flowers, the quills being red and opening orange; late Oct–Nov; the distinctive foliage is a jagged grey-green; and its' delicate-looking spider-like flowers appear to contradict their frost-resistance and this cultivar's hardiness as a garden perennial and long-lasting cut flower. Listed as a best buy by Which? Gardening, this is a special plant.

'Burnt Orange'

'Buxton Ruby' individual flower

'Buxton Ruby'; ↕40cm; small 1cm single red flowers with a yellow button centre; Nov; a bushy plant with small dark leaves and stems, appear up to Christmas if the weather is mild.

Found as an unnamed plant at Woottens of Wenhaston by HPS member Brenda Reed. Named after the Norfolk village where she lives, ruby being self explanatory. There is reference by Margery Fish to a French plant she calls 'Tiny', barely a foot high, covered in tiny crimson flowers, with a golden eye.

'Buxton Ruby' flower spray

'Capel Manor'

'Buxton Ruby' habit

'Capel Manor'; 2006 21d Y; ↕100–130cm; 7.5cm strongly-scented double flowers, with touches of gold fading to a deep buff-cream, having 50% quilled petals, opening from coppery buds; Oct–Nov; has a strong vigorous but lax plant growth, with leaves that redden in the autumn.

A very old hardy variety found growing for many years in the borders of Capel Manor Hortcultural College, the plants look great when grown through a small obelisk for support. Resembles 'Emperor of China' in habit and flower shape.

'Carmine Blush'

'Carmine Blush'; RHS AGM 2009; 21d LP; ↕60–90cm; 4–6.5cm flowers are mid-pink with blue tones creating a highly floriferous plant; Oct–Dec; and forms a compact attractive bush.

This is a seedling selected by prevailing weather conditions in 1981 by Bob Brown of Cotswold Garden Flowers who says it is *"utterly weatherproof"*.

Carmine Blush' habit

'Chelsea Physic Garden'

'Chelsea Physic Garden'; ↕115cm; 6cm double red-bronze flowers with a gold reverse that are very weatherproof; Nov; plants benefit from staking in a windy site. Thanks go to Nottcutts plant propagator Ivan Dickings for passing on a plant that came down through the Ablett family. Frank Ablett died in 1957 aged 95 and passed it on to his grandson making this cultivar traceable for at least 100 years.

'Chelsea Physic Garden' flower spray

'Christmas'; ↕110cm; large, duplex dark-red flowers, 7.5cm across, with a white central ring, that are scented; foliage is grey; similar cultivar to 'Royal Command'. CWW

'Christmas'

'Citronella'; ↕90cm; 5-7cm soft clear-yellow, fragrant double flowers that look luminous in autumn borders; Aug–Oct; makes an excellent cut flower. CWW
A Karl Foerster nursery introduction, who released it in 1977, seven years after his death.

'Citronella'

'Clara Curtis'

'Clara Curtis' habit

'Clara Curtis'; 2006 21d LP; ↕86cm; large 6cm pale-pink flowers stand out well from a yellow heart though flowers are not entirely weatherproof; late-Aug–mid-Oct; forms a compact clump with small, very divided leaves borne on reddish stems. CWW
'Clara Curtis' is one of the original Rubellums raised by Amos Perry in 1939 and has floral branches which provide an exquisite bouquet of cut flowers.

'Colsterworth'; ↕60–80cm; 4.5cm single pink-mauve anemone-type flowers; mid-Oct–Nov.
Found as a plant in the Lincolnshire village of Colsterworth and whose true name has been lost. Norwell Nurseries say it has proved itself both healthy and hardy over many winters. The compact habit makes it suitable for growing in pots.

'Clara Curtis' spray

'Colsterworth'

'Constable'

'Corinna'

'Constable'; ↕45cm; 2.5cm multiple small double yellow flowers; Oct; a relatively modern cushion which has proved to be hardy.

The raiser is possibly Cleangro UK, who dissolved in 2012, having been bought out by Dutch wholesale chrysanthemum company Van Zanten BV some years earlier.

'Corinna' flower spray

'Constable' plant habit

'Corinna'; ↕60–85cm; 5cm scented flowers, duplex pink anemone with a white inner ring; Oct–Nov; forms a neat mound with dark stems and is very hardy. Raised by Karl Foerster and introduced in 1958.

'Corinna' plant habit

'Cottage Apricot'
flower spray

'Cottage Apricot' (Cottage Bronze, Apricot); 2006 21d B; ↕76cm; 6cm single, deep-apricot flowers with a yellow inner ring; late-Oct; slow to start growing but then romps away to make large clumps.

Its' history is unknown, however, as Margery Fish once wrote (Cottage Garden Flowers), *'There are certain rather ordinary, good-tempered chrysanthemums that have become to be known as 'Cottage Pink' or 'Cottage Bronze' because at one time they were found in every cottage garden.'*

'Cottage Apricot'

'Cottage Apricot'
in a garden
border with
artemisia

'Cottage Lemon'

'Cottage Lemon' plant habit

'Cottage Lemon'; ↕125cm; 5cm soft and warm yellow duplex flowers with wide petals that open from coppery buds tinged red; Oct–Nov; the frost-resistant flowers last a long time when cut for indoors.

'Cottage Yellow' (Margery Fish); ↕70cm; 4cm single yellow flowers which bunch at the end of the stems on short pedicels and are attractive to bees; mid-Oct; the plant habit is lax.

This form came from Mrs Seager's uncle's cottage in the village of Hartland, Devon. Her father moved from Collinwood London, to Devon prior to WW2 so the plant has been known since the 1950's. Margery Fish wrote in Cottage Garden Flowers, *'The old 'Cottage Yellow' is not very tall and is a pleasant not too strident colour.'* Similarities exist with 'Sarah's Yellow'.

'Cottage Yellow'

'Cottage Yellow' flower spray

'Cousin Joan'

'Daniel Cooper'

'Cousin Joan'; RHS AGM 2012; 2006 21d DR; ↕140cm; 6cm single bright red-purple flowers with a white single ring; floriferous and strongly sweet-scented; Oct–Nov; it has large-leaved clean, greyish foliage and is attractive to bees.

Found by Hertfordshire HPS member Janet Horton, in her elderly cousin's Harrow garden and grown there for many years. This very hardy cultivar has survived with not much attention, even after a frost. The front cover shows a macro image of this lovely flower, by John McCormack.

'Daniel Cooper'; RHS AGM 2012; ↕85cm; 5cm single, bright cerise-pink flowers; Sep–Oct; forms a nice shape with stiff, upright stems making it an excellent plant for the border. The leaf is not a typical Rubellum having very broad leaves which redden in autumn.

A seedling from 'Clara Curtis' raised by Mr Anthony Wright of Collinwood Nursery and named after his grandson, 1992.

'Dernier Soleil' ('Last Sun'); ↕120cm; 5cm single golden-yellow-centred petals tipped with burnt orange which give a warm effect; end Jul–Nov.

'Dernier Soleil'

'Daniel Cooper' habit

An old French variety that is very early and extremely long flowering and useful as a cut flower. French nurserymen recommend cutting the stems down by half in early summer to produce a more compact and floriferous effect. Thierry Delabroye has raised a white form of this cultivar called 'Dernier Soleil Blanc' and a seedling form with orange-yellow double pompons called 'Coup de Soleil'.

'**Dixter Orange**'; ↕80cm; 4.5cm a mass of double orange pompon flowers; Sep–Nov. CWW

This cultivar is one of the late Christopher Lloyd's recommended plants of Great Dixter garden, another is 'Dixter Pink'; regrettably suffers badly from white rust.

'Dixter Orange'

'**Doctor Tom Parr**'; (Dr. Bob Parr, Rob Roy); 2006 21c DS; ↕70cm; 3.5cm madder-rose-coloured pompon petals with gold highlights fading to buff, which shorten at the flat centre top; Sep–Oct; can be used to support plants such as 'Emperor of China'. CWW

A sport of 'Anastasia' described in 'Gardener's Chronicle' October 1968 04 Vol 164 by Barbara Morrison. Margery Fish in her book *'Cottage Garden Flowers'* wrote *"It is a shame that so many of these old hardy chrysanthemums have disappeared .... There is one of these pompons that seems to be a great favourite judging by the number of names it has. It is a pinkish-bronze, almost rose-madder .... To me, it is 'Dr Tom Parr' ...."*

'Doctor Tom Parr'

'Duchess of Edinburgh'

'**Duchess of Edinburgh**'; 2006 21d R; ↕60cm; 5cm flowers are a rich coppery-red single duplex; Sep–Oct; the large leaves redden in autumn; stems can flop due to the heavy flowers atop the thin stems. CWW

Raised by Amos Perry and included in his 1948 catalogue, it received an Award of Merit that same year.

'Dulwich Pink'

'**Dulwich Pink**'; RHS AGM 2012; ↕70cm; 6cm single bright mid-pink duplex flowers with darker buds; flowers very weather resistant; Oct–Nov; forms a pleasing much-branched bush giving a tapestry of changing pinks. CWW

'Dulwich Pink' came from Dulwich Park, London, via psychotherapist Professor Isaac Marks where it was grown in the winter garden that he designed in 2001.

'Edmund Brown'

'Edmund Brown'; ↕55cm; 6cm glowing deep chestnut duplex flowers; Oct–Nov; forms a low dome.
Raised and introduced by Bob Brown and named after his son.

'E.H. Wilson'; ↕110cm; 4cm highly scented duplex cream flowers contrast with the dark stems in profusion; late-Nov; a fabulous cut flower, the multi-headed flower stems acting like a large gypsophila, filling in amongst other stems in a vase; clumps quickly even after mild but very wet winters.
Probably introduced by plant hunter Ernest Wilson when he was collecting for the Arnold Arboretum, and which may in fact be a species. It has been kept by Paul Pearn, Rainbow Borders, Isle of Man, for many years, who obtained it from Bill Archer, who was given this cultivar by Miss Pole, a long-running chair of the early HPS.

'Early Yellow'

'Early Yellow'; ↕80cm; 4.5cm single, pale sulphur-yellow duplex flowers with large golden centre; end Aug–Nov; strong upright growth; very hardy with a long flowering time, in some areas even from July.
Predating 1960.

'Early Yellow' flower spray

'E.H. Wilson'

'Early Yellow' garden habit

'Edelweiss'; ↕120cm; pale champagne-pink buds open to large 8.5cm pink fading to white, duplex flowers with shorter petals at the green-eyed centre reminiscent of an edelweiss or shasta daisy; regrettably damaged by frost and heavy rain; Sep–mid-Nov; has a lax habit. CWW
A lovely plant which Norwell Nurseries describes as one of the best large whites.

'Edelweiss'

'Elaine's Hardy'

'Elaine's Hardy'; ↕60cm; 6cm apricot buds opening to a white single; Oct–Nov; foliage reddening as it ages.

'Emperor of China' (Cottage Pink); 2006 21f LP; ↕140cm; 7.5cm double flowers, with silver-pink quilled petals, flushed with purple; swirls in the middle; forms secondary buds on short stems; late-Oct–Nov; a very tough, floppy plant, with large, broad, veined leaves that redden in the cold, contrast well with the flowers; benefits from support when flower stems are weighed down by rain.

'Emperor of China'

This is an old variety, mentioned by William Robinson in a book dated circa. 1880.

'Esther'; 2006 21d LP; ↕80cm; 7cm apricot-peach petals on a double flower that are shorter towards the centre giving a 'shaggy' effect; Aug–Oct; forms a slightly floppy mound. CWW
Raised by Joe Sharman of Monksilver Nursery in the 1990s from seed of a Rubellum; he writes it starts flowering from early July.

'Esther'

'Fellbacher Wein'

'Fellbacher Wein'; ↕60cm; 5cm duplex flowers in red; Sep–Oct; an upright bush. CWW
Raised in Germany, probably named for the wine of the Fellbacher wine garden; the breeder is unknown but has been listed as both the Swiss breeder Carl Ludwig Frikart and German breeder Pfizer.

'Folksong'

'Folksong'; ↕100cm; 5cm double-flowered lemon-yellow cultivar reminiscent of a pompon dahlia, similar to 'Citronella', backs of the unopened petals have a lime tinge; Sep–early-Nov; beautifully scented flowers of honey and lemon; foliage is attractive.
Breeder unknown, but propagated by the Aylings who ran Kingsley nursery in Kingsley, Hampshire.

'Freds Yellow' garden habit

'Freds Yellow'; ↕60cm; 5cm wide bright yellow duplex flowers; Sep–Nov; a long-flowering floriferous plant which never looks untidy, it forms a bushy-mounded plant with dark leaves and stems.
Grown at Hill Close Gardens, this cultivar was found in a garden in Warwick.

'Freds Yellow' spray

'Freds Yellow'

'French Rose'; ↕100cm; 5cm clear-pink single flowers; Sep–Oct; possibly a good seedling of 'Clara Curtis'. CWW

'French Rose'

Habit of 'Goldengreenheart'

'Goldengreenheart'

'Goldengreenheart'; RHS AGM 2012; 2006 21d LB; ↕120cm; 4cm single duplex weather-resistant flowers in a green-gold colour; late Oct–Nov; this is a very hardy stiff upright plant.
A seedling raised by Bob Brown of Cotswold Garden Flowers who writes it can still be looking good at Christmas.

'Hebe'; ↕80cm; 6cm single pale-pink flowers with a yellow-green heart and central white ring; Sep–Nov; an easy reliable form, with a branching habit, suitable for cutting.
A more compact form of 'Innocence' hailing from what is today known as the Nikita Botanical Gardens – National Scientific Centre of Russian Academy of Sciences (NBG-NSC), one of the oldest research institutions in the Crimea, established in 1812. They continue to release new cold hardy cultivars and have a dedicated hardy chrysanthemum garden.

'Grandchild'

'Grandchild'; RHS AGM 2009; 1973 21c P; ↕45cm; 5cm double cushion flowers of a bright mauve-pink; Aug–Sep; a good plant for the front of the border or pots, it has dark green rounded leaves. CWW Submitted to the RHS 1979 trial by Orpington nurseries giving the origin as Bristol Nurseries, USA.

'Grandchild' habit

'Hebe'

'Helen Ward'; ↕110cm; 4cm dusky coral-crimson semi-double flowers that age to a pale rose-madder; Sep–Oct; excellent healthy foliage. Raised by Dr Andrew Ward of Norwell Nurseries and named for his wife; another seedling from a group of crosses using 'Dr Tom Parr' as the female parent.

'Helen Ward'

'Herbstrose' (Hollyhock); ↕100cm; 7cm single pink flowers; forms a low, compact floriferous mound.
A Schleipfer crossing with the species *Chrysanthemum arcticum*.

somewhat floppy but makes a very pretty front of border plant. CWW
Raised by brothers Jonas & Thomas Johnson, Tibshelf, UK in 1956 and included in the 1960 RHS trial having been given an award of merit in 1957.

'Herbstrose'

'Imp' flower spray

'Imp'; RHS AGM 2012; 2006 21e R; ↕60cm; 4cm chestnut-crimson red, spherical double flowers that fade to bronze; Aug–Sep; has dark green leaves and can be

'Imp'

'Imp' garden habit

'Innocence'

'Innocence'; RHS AGM 2012; ↕90cm; 6cm single pale-pink flowers with a white inner ring and green spot in the centre; Oct–Nov; highly floriferous with large leaves that redden in autumn, the bees love this typical Rubellum type, which may flop a bit after rain.
Raised in France as 'L'innocence' and anglicised to 'Innocence'. Makes a great cut flower; similar to 'Aunt Millicent'.

'Janet South'; RHS AGM 2006; 21d P; ↕145cm; pink duplex 8cm perfectly formed flowers opening from darker pink buds, with a small inner white ring; Oct–Nov; a strong and tall fairly upright plant with large glossy dark green leaves; clumps up quickly if a mild winter; a sweetly-scented plant, it is a strong grower covered in flowers which attract insects. CWW
Grown as an informal hedge alongside HPS member Janet South's drive near Pershore, Worcestershire, prior to them moving in.

'Janet South'

'Jante Wells'

'Jante Wells' flower spray

'Jante Wells'; RHS AGM 2012; 1937 28 Y; ↕80-100cm; 4cm dainty bright yellow pompon; mid-Sep–Nov; forming a rounded branching dome with dark green leaves making a lovely front of border plant. It was once extensively used as an autumn bedding plant during the 60's in London parks and gardens. CWW
Named after Ben Well's daugher of Wells of Mertsham nursery and launched in 1938. 'Judith Anderson' from Bristol Nurseries, Connecticut, USA is similar.

'Jolie Rose' ('Pretty Rose'); ↕60–75cm; 4.5cm medium-sized rose-pink duplex flowers with a paler white inner ring; Oct–Nov; great for bouquets.
Of unknown origin, sold by Bob Brown of Cotswold Garden Flowers.

'Jolie Rose'

'Julia'; ↕60cm; 3cm palest-pink pompon flowers ageing to white; Sep–Nov; a compact and stable plant perfect in bouquets, and is quick to clump up. CWW
Possibly a German-bred cultivar.

'Julia'

'Julia Peterson'; ↕80cm; 2.5cm double deep-mauve-magenta flowers clustered atop branching stems; flowers are scented; Sep–Nov. CWW
Bred by Clive Hester in Gloucestershire.

'Julia Peterson'

'Julie Lagravère'; ↕45cm; small 1cm dark red double poms with a gold reverse and flat top flower; late-Oct–Nov; the small dullish green leaves redden in autumn. CWW
Bred by August Bonamy in 1821 in France when George IV was on the throne.

Killerton is a national trust property in Devon where John Veitch was head gardener and where he began the famous Veitch Nurseries. This cultivar resembles a greenhouse exhibition type in flower, ie it looks fully double until the flowers are very mature, in late November.

'Killerton Tangerine' (Killerton Orange); ↕130cm; large 7cm semi-double flowers in a dark orange colour; flowering Oct–Dec; has been known to succumb to eelworm. CWW

'Kleiner Bernstein'; ↕70cm; 7cm orange with duplex flowers that have a unique dusky orange glow; Sep–Nov; a short compact cultivar. CWW
Background unknown, but possibly raised by Töpperwein 1961.

'Lady in Pink'

'Lady in Pink' ('Pink Progression', 'Pink Procession') 2006 21d P; ↕70cm; 6.5cm pale-pink flowers in a single row, long pointed petals with inner white ring; Oct–Nov; extremely floriferous; 'Lady in Pink' is a reliable dome-shaped plant. CWW
A true Rubellum raised by Amos Perry in 1952.

'Lady in Pink' plant habit

'Leo'; RHS AGM 2012; 21b LB; ↕90cm; small 4cm yellow pompons with a bronze eye; Oct; forming a domed bush. CWW
Raised by Joe Sharman of Monksilver Nursery, and not to be confused with Chrysanthemum 'Spartan Leo', of the Spartan Series developed by Jack Woolman. 'Leo' is Latin for 'lion'.

'Leo'

'Lindie'

'Lindie'; ↕90cm; 8cm flowers with lemon quilled petals giving this cultivar a very pretty 'spider-like' appearance; late Oct–Nov; its' growth is somewhat lax in wet weather.

'Lucy Simpson'

'Lucy Simpson'; 2006 21d LB; ↕76cm; 5cm rich bronze-buff duplex flowers, with a light yellow ring at the centre; mid-Sep–Oct; plants have a loose relaxed growth and finely divided foliage.
An Otley Korean raised by Fred Simpson in 1938.

'Lucy Simpson' flower spray

'Mandarin'; ↕70cm; double flowers are 6.5cm with gold tints coral, salmon, copper; Sep–Nov. CWW
Found in Wells catalogue in 1939.

'Mandarine'; ↕70cm; 6.5cm double orange flowers; Sep–Oct. CWW
From Prague Botanic Garden, but breeder/raiser unknown; unfortunately an example of double-naming. Introduced to the UK by collection holder Judy Barker.

'Mandarine'

'Margery Fish'

'Margery Fish' ('Cottage Yellow', Sarah's Yellow); ↕120cm; bright golden-yellow semi-double 6cm flowers; Oct–Nov.
Named for famed plantswoman and gardening author Margery Fish of East Lambrook Manor Gardens in Somerset; may be a re-named form.

'Marion'; 1996 21d B; ↕90cm; 6.5cm glowing semi-quilled duplex chestnut-red flowers with a yellow inner ring; mid-Oct–Nov; habit is somewhat lax. CWW
Found in Home Meadow catalogue and previously named in a 1980's Orpington catalogue who are most likely the raiser of this cultivar.

'Marion'

'Mary'

'Mary' plant habit

'Mary'; 2006 21f LY; ↕66cm; 8cm part-quilled duplex cream flowers; mid-Sep–Oct. CWW

Raised in Holland for the cut flower trade possibly as early as 1949; given mention in the September 1952 RHS Journal.

'Mary Stoker' plant habit

'Mary Stoker'

'Mary Stoker'; 2006 21d LB; ↕100cm; stunning and unusual shade of creamy yellow-apricot single flowers, 8cm across; Sep–Oct; the leaves redden in autumn and the plant has a running rootstock. CWW

A true Rubellum, the breeder was Amos Perry who released it in 1942.

'Mavis'

'Mavis' plant habit

'Mavis'; 1971 28a P (now re-classified under section 21, but before 2006 under section 28); ↕66cm; 5cm pompon flowers which are a mauve-pink with a darker contrasting centre; late Aug–Sep; has a bushy upright habit. CWW

Raised by Joseph and Thomas Johnson, The Nurseries, Tibshelf, Derby, not now trading but who were once prolific show chrysanthemum breeders.

'Mavis Smith' plant habit

'Mavis Smith'

'Mavis Smith'; ↕135cm; large 9cm mid-pink flowers with quilled petals; late Oct–Nov; a vigorous, healthy addition for the back of the border; it is beautifully scented of honey and makes a great cut flower having strong upright growth; clumps very quickly.

Discovered by HPS member Mavis Smith in a garden in Elmswell, Suffolk.

'Mei-Kyo'; RHS AGM 2012; 2006 21d P; ↕75cm; 3cm dainty, weatherproof, semi-pompon flowers of mauve-pink; Oct–Nov; an upright self-supporting plant it bears small leaves; a good cut flower it gives great late colour to the border.

'Mei-Kyo' was sent to nurseryman Will Ingwersen in the 1950's from Japan, in a matchbox. The name means 'Treasure of Kyoto' where the Kyoto Imperial garden is to be found. Named sports include 'Nantderry Sunshine' (yellow), 'Purleigh White' (white) and 'Bronze Elegance' (bronze).

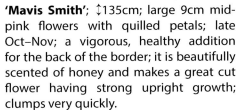

ei-Kyo' plant habit

'Mei-Kyo'

'Menuet'; ↕85cm; 3cm, tiny bronze-orange semi-pom flowers; Nov–Dec; small bushy dome. CWW

Introduced from the Conservatoire Nationale du Chrysanthème by Paul LeMaire. 'President Ozaka' reverts to this.

'Menuet'

'Mrs Jessie Cooper'; RHS AGM 2012; 2006 21d Pu; ↕110cm; 7.5cm large, single bright-cerise-pink blooms with a small white central ring; late Oct–Dec; with shiny thick tri-lobate leaves, this lovely late-flowering, self-supporting cultivar, takes whatever the weather throws at it Nurseryman Dr Andrew Ward describes this cultivar as *"One of the toughest, virtually indestructible even on clay!"*

'Mrs Jessie Cooper'

'Mrs Jessie Cooper' flower spray

'Mrs Jessie Cooper Number Two' ('Rose Madder'); ↕140cm; 8cm duplex rose-madder-coloured flowers with a white central ring; Nov.

The background is unverified, and the plant resembles 'Rose Madder' from Bob Brown's Cotswold Garden Plants.

'Mrs Jessie Cooper Number Two'

'Nancy Perry'; 2006 21d DP; ↕60cm; the 8cm duplex flowers are an old rose colour fading to a strawberry pink; mid-Sep–Oct; a tough, upright self-supporting plant with rather thick stems and large leaves which redden in autumn. CWW
Raised by Amos Perry in 1945 and a true Rubellum form.

'Nantyderry Sunshine'
showing reversion and habit

A yellow sport of 'Mei-Kyo', it was found in the garden of Welsh garden TV presenter Mrs Rose Clay in 1989; sections can revert as picture above shows.

'Nancy Perry'

'Old Norwell'; ↕100cm; 5cm duplex flowers of a rain-washed coral-salmon; Oct–Nov.
Raised by Dr Andrew Ward of Norwell Nurseries and bred from Dr Tom Parr, part of a collection that has a floriferous nature, old fashioned dusky tones and healthy foliage. Andrew writes on his website *"It must be very good for us to have put our name to it."*

'Old Norwell'

'Nantyderry Sunshine'; RHS AGM 1996; 2006 21f Y; ↕90cm; small 3cm bright yellow semi-pompon flowers with a yellow centre; mid-Oct–Nov; forms a strong rounded bushy plant with strong winter basal growth; it is sufficiently robust to be planted as an informal hedge which turns yellow in autumn.

'Nantyderry Sunshine'

'Paul Boissier'; 2006 21d B; ↕90cm; 5.5cm semi-double flowers with sharp pointed petals in a rich orange-bronze colour with greenish tints at the swirled centre on opening; mid-Oct–Nov; can be somewhat floppy in habit, but in a pleasantly relaxed way. CWW

'Paul Boissier' relaxed habit

A true Perry's Rubellum, raised and released in 1945 by Amos Perry, which received an award of merit from the RHS in 1948 (now rescinded) following a field trial of Rubellums and Koreans. It was likely named after Paul Boissier, a headmaster at the exclusive Middlesex private boarding school at Harrow. Another Perry chrysanthemum, described as pale apricot-yellow-flushed rose, was named 'Dorothy Boissier' in 1942, after Paul Boissier's wife Dorothy.

'Paul Boissier'

'Peggy'

'Peggy'; ↕50cm; 6cm soft peach-coral double flowers; Sep–Oct; this pretty plant has an open and relaxed growth habit. CWW

Sold by Home Meadow Nursery of Woodbridge in 2000.

'Penny's Yellow'

'Penny's Yellow' ('Richard's Yellow'); ↕122cm; 6.5cm bright yellow, double clustered flowers, with a greenish centre; late Oct–Nov; hardy tough stems that can flop a bit, has large leaves which redden in autumn, shrugs off slugs and winter wet forming a strong footprint in the ground and makes a welcome late burst of colour in the garden.

HPS member Penny Hay bought this form originally as an unnamed cultivar from The Telegraph newspaper years ago and introduced it to a nursery who subsequently propagated it for sale.

'Perry's Peach'

'Perry's Peach'; RHS AGM 2009; 2006 21d LS; ↕75cm; 6.5cm soft peach-pink single flowers whose duplex petals have a cream-yellow central ring; Sep–Oct; forms a well-branched mound covered in upward facing flowers which always look tidy, ie as one flower fades, the next appears to cover the fading flower; also seems to shrug off slugs and the leaves occasionally redden in autumn; an all round excellent cultivar. CWW

'Perry's Peach' has no known connection to the 'Rubellums' bred by Amos Perry, Enfield. It was found as an un-named form in an old garden in Whitby around 1980 and called after the finders - a Pat and Bill Perry of Perry's Plants, whose son Richard now runs the nursery turned garden centre called 'The River Gardens'.

'Picasso'; ↕60cm; 4cm double pompon flowers in a soft peach colour with a darker centre, fading to buff and dark peach buds; Oct–Nov; forms a dense dome with weather-resistant flowers, this cushion chrysanthemum may require some winter protection (H3). CWW

'Picasso' was entered by Yoder Toddington into an RHS trial from 2001 so likely from their breeding stable. They developed a whole range named after the Old Masters such as Rembrandt, Turner, Gauguin, Cezanne, Vermeer and so on. This cultivar is named for the great 20th century Spanish artist Pablo Picasso who painted a still life of cut flower chrysanthemums at the age of 20 that is still famous today.

'Picasso'

'Picasso' dome habit

'Poesie'

'Poesie'; ↕110cm; 5cm creamy-white duplex, very rounded scented flowers that turn pink when pollinated, and mature to white; Sep–Nov; long-flowering and extremely hardy.

Introduced to the UK via Norwell Nurseries and recommended for its enormous wealth of flowers, hardiness and stability, it is said to last for weeks as a cut flower. It was discovered by Wolfgang Kautz, of Potsdam Nursery, in a Romanian village among the Carpathian mountains. An un-named cultivar, the German nurseryman propagated and introduced it in 2002 as 'Poesie' which translates to 'poetry'. In 2004 it received an ISU award from the International Hardy Plant Union. French nurseryman Thierry Delabroye selected a pink-infused form from this which he called 'Poésie Rose'.

'President Ozaka'; 85cm; 3cm very tiny semi-pompon flowers of a very bright yellow; Nov–Dec; the densely-branched plants have dark green leaves and have proven to be very tough and weatherproof, creating a novel garden plant that brings a breath of fresh air at a time when little else is in flower with the bonus of behaving well as a cut flower.

This novelty came from the Conservatoire National du Chrysanthème Paul Lemaire (National Museum of the Chrysanthemum), in Saint-Jean-le-Braye, whose mission is to collect old and rare varieties, ensuring their preservation.

'President Ozaka'

'Purleigh White'; 2006 21d OC (LP); ↕85cm; pink buds open to give small 3cm white semi-pompon flowers that age to a soft pink with a small yellow eye on maturity; Oct–Nov; a sport of 'Mei-Kyo' this cultivar sometimes reverts; it forms a dense branched dome with small leaves and makes a good support and foil for other plants. CWW

Introduced in 1988 by Mr Don Nowell who found the white sport and named it for his home town of Purleigh in Essex.

'Ray's Red'

'Ray's Red'; ↕60cm; small paprika-red pompon flowers 2.5cm across that eventually develop a tiny yellow eye; late Sep–Nov; compact growth covered in flowers and an easy form to grow.

The name is informal and was named for highly respected Nottingham gardener Ray Cobb, a past holder of the Plant Heritage National Collection® of crocus as well as a snowdrop expert. Introduced by Norwell Nurseries.

'Purleigh White'

'Red Elite'

'Red Elite'; 1971 29d R; ↕50cm; 5cm flowers in a bright-red duplex form; Sep–Oct; it is an upright plant with strong stems.

Raised by Elm House (mail order nursery), Wisbech as part of their Elite range released in 1971 which also included 'Pink Elite', 'Dark Elite' and 'Bronze Elite'.

'Purleigh White'

'Rhumba'; ↕55cm; 5m single peach flowers; Sep–Nov; forms a neat cushion-like plant. CWW
Bred by American landscape designer, Rika Bronsther.

'Rhumba'

'Romantica'; ↕100cm; 3cm soft-pink semi-pompon flowers fading to cream with a darker centre.
Of German origin, Norwell Nurseries describes it as rather like a taller, darker 'Julia'.

'Romantica'

'Rose Madder'; ↕65cm; bright pink-red duplex flowers, 5cm across; mid-Sep–Oct; an upright self-supporting plant.
Raised by Bob Brown of Cotswold Garden Flowers who describes the flowers as scented. Flowers are comparable to Mrs Jessie Cooper No. 2

'Rosetta'

'Rosetta'; ↕70cm; lovely 6cm soft pink double flowers with a 'smoked-salmon' cast giving a lovely two-tone effect as it ages to white; mid-Aug–Oct; is an extremely early and sturdy plant; deadhead later to stop the retained old brown flowers from marring the new ones. CWW
Raised in France, nurseryman Thierry Delabroye writes his selection 'Pompon Girl' is similar.

'Rose Madder'

'Röter Spray' (Schleipfer's 'Red Spray'); ↕80cm; 6cm duplex raspberry-purple flowers with a yellow centre – this is a unique form that looks like it has been darned in purple threads; Sep–Nov; very healthy foliage.

Possibly originates from the Neusäß nursery of German plant breeder Eugen Schleipfer, near Augsburg.

'Röter Spray'

'Royal Command'; ↕95cm; 7cm glossy deep-red duplex flowers; late Oct–Nov; self-supporting plant with greyish leaves. Raised and introduced by Amos Perry in 1949 – a true Rubellum.

'Royal Command' plant habit

'Royal Command'

'Ruby Mound'; RHS AGM 2005; 1996 21c DR; ↕115cm; 6cm fabulous deep-maroon double flowers; mid-Sep–Nov; initially self-supporting 'cushion' plant but requiring support once established, 'Ruby Mound' is suited to being cut, gives a pleasing shape, and the flowers literally 'sparkle with diamonds' after a rainfall. CWW

Raised by Dick Lehman of Minnesota USA in the 1950s, a 'Minnesota Mum™', that has stood the test of time in our British climate and considered an 'absolute must' for the garden by hardy chrysanthemum expert Andrew Ward. The pigment penetrates the petals which avoids faded flowers – Faribault Growers Inc, 'Home of Mums of Minnesota' today still say *"Far ahead of anything we have seen in red cushion."*

'Ruby Mound'

'Ruby Raynor' loose bush habit

'Ruby Raynor'; RHS AGM 2007; 2006 21c LB; ↕75cm; 5cm double flowers in a very bright golden-yellow flushed with bronze-coppery centres; Sep–Oct; forms a loose bush with thick stems. CWW

The name 'Ruby Raynor' confuses customers expecting it to be ruby-red in colour. Found in an old Elm House catalogue and likely related to cultivars 'Dick Raynor', 'Guy Raynor', 'Kip Raynor', 'Laura Raynor', 'Nell Raynor' and 'Sid Raynor' all released in 1965. The breeder was LR Emmans, author of 'Chrysanthemums for the Beginner', published by Elm House Nurseries in 1957. A beautiful cultivar that has stood the test of time.

'Rumplestilzchen'; 2006 21d R; ↕70cm; 4cm duplex flowers, open a bronze-orange but redden to a rusty-red with a yellow inner ring as the nights get longer and colder; Aug–Nov; one of the earliest to flower; forms a loose bush. CWW

Origin unknown but possibly a Karl Foerster plant, whose German name is a mythical character from the 18th century fairy tales of the Brothers Grimm. (p26)

'Ruby Raynor'

'Rumplestilzchen'

'Ruth Buckley'; ↕70cm; 4cm single, lemon-yellow flowers, resembling 'Early Yellow' but tougher; Sep–Nov; an upright self-supporting plant with a long flowering period that thrives on little attention and the slugs leave her alone.

Submitted by the late Ruth Buckley, Conservation Officer for the HPS Shropshire group and propagated by them.

'Sea Urchin'

'Ruth Buckley'

'Sea Urchin'; RHS AGM 2005; 1996 21f LY; ↕60cm; amazing 7cm fully-quilled lemon-yellow petals on a loose cushioned double flower; Sep–Oct; hardiness is H3 but it is worth either growing in a pot or covering in winter.

Raised in the 'Mums from Minnesota™' programme and still sold by Faribault Growers today. Orpington Nurseries used to sell this in 1980.

'Sarah's Yellow'

'Sea Urchin' cushion habit

'Sarah's Yellow' ('Cottage Yellow', 'Margery Fish'); ↕80cm; 5cm bright yellow duplex flowers which bunch at the end of the stems; Oct–Nov; upright self-supporting very hardy plant that is slug resistant – adds a bright splash of colour at the end of the season.

'Sheffield Pink' used as a cut flower

'Sheffield Pink' ('Sheffield', 'Hillside Pink', 'Single Apricot'); ↕50cm; 6cm single soft-pink-apricot daisies; Oct; though a strong clean grower the flowers are not weather resistant; said to be attractive to butterflies and suitable to grow in a tub. CWW

An old American cultivar, possibly a mutation from 'Clara Curtis' and used by New York breeder Rika Bronsther to produce hardiness in her landscape range, the *Chrysanthemum* Autumn Crescendo™ Series, named after dances eg 'Rhumba'.

'Sheffield Pink' plant habit

'Selly Oak Purple'; ↕75cm; 7.5cm single pink flowers; Oct–Nov; forms a broad spreading bush.

Found in a Selly Oak (Birmingham) churchyard happily spreading itself around.

'Selly Oak Purple';

'Šlapanická Eliška'

'Šlapanická Eliška'; ↕75cm; 6cm red single flowers; Oct–Nov; self-supporting, tough weather-proof plant.

Sent by Prague Botanic Gardens, and introduced to the UK by collection holder Judy Barker.

'Šlapanická Heda'; ↕75cm; 6cm single pink flowers; Oct–Nov; self-supporting, tough weather-proof plant with vigorous root system.

Sent by Prague Botanic Gardens, and introduced to the UK by collection holder Judy Barker.

'Šlapanická Eliška' plant habit

'Šlapanická Heda' plant habit

'Šlapanická Vladěnka'

'Spartan Canary'

'Šlapanická Vladěnka'; ↕100cm; 5cm soft-bronze single flowers; Oct–Nov; self-supporting, tough weather-proof plant.
Sent by Prague Botanic Gardens, and introduced to the UK by collection holder Judy Barker.

'Spartan Canary'; RHS AGM 2012; 2006 21c LB; ↕75cm; darker buds precede 5cm double yellow-bronze flowers; Sep-Oct. CWW
One colour from a wide range bred by Woolmans, said to be winter hardy, but growing best in patio pots. Other colours in the Spartan range include 'Display', 'Linnet', 'Seagull', 'Leo', 'Raspberry', and 'Star'.

'Starlet'; RHS AGM 2012; 1996 21f LB; ↕55cm; lovely 5cm flowers with several layers of duplex-spoon petals in a light bronze; Aug–Sep; forms a loose spreading dome and will grow in pots; attractive to bees. CWW
Raised between 1950–1960 from the 'Mums from Minnesota™' programme and still found in the Faribault catalogue today. 'Yellow Starlet', a cheerful plant with a long flowering period, is a sport from this cultivar.

'Starlet'

'Stratford Pink'; 2006 21d LPu; ↕115cm; large 8cm single pink 'gappy' flowers with a white inner ring; Sep–Nov; having healthy foliage, the leaves redden in autumn on this strong and sturdy plant. Possibly a Woolman's plant.

'Stratford Pink'

'Suffolk Pink'; 2006 21d P; ↕120cm; 6cm much-branched single dark-pink flowers aging to a dusky pink with a tiny white central ring; Oct–Nov; foliage is very healthy.

An unknown cultivar found in an old garden in Sudbury, Suffolk and named for the county of Suffolk.

'Suffolk Pink' branched plant habit

'Suffolk Pink'

'Sweetheart Pink'; ↕120cm; two-tone soft-pink 9cm perfect double flowers reminiscent of a dahlia, open from peachy pink buds; Sep–Nov; a favourite of Dr Andrew Ward, 'Sweetheart Pink' is very long flowering, making a great cut flower.

'Sweetheart Pink' flower spray

A Johnson brothers introduction from 1940, found growing in the garden of Elisabeth Wakeland Smith for over fifty years, by Sarah Cook, iris collection holder.

'Sweetheart Pink'

'Syllabub' in bud

'Syllabub' dome-shaped habit

'Syllabub'; ↕50cm; 5cm flower with beautiful quilled, spoon-tipped petals, anemone-centred and mauve-pink; Sep–Oct; makes a rounded or dome-shaped plant that is hardiness H3 but 'Syllabub' is certainly worth protecting in winter to ensure its increased survival. CWW

Raised by Cleangro Ltd, who entered it into the 2001 RHS trial. 'Syllabub Purple', also a garden hardy plant, was a mutation from this that occurred at Cleangro and was patented by Keith Lintott in 2005 (later assigned to Van Zanten 2011).

'Syllabub'

'Tapestry Rose'

'Tapestry Rose'; ↕95cm; small 5cm rose-pink single flowers with green dot at centre; Sep–Oct; the finely divided greyish foliage is covered in a short but late burst of autumn colour that welcomes beneficial insects; a relaxed, some say floppy, multi-stemmed plant that *"roots like couch grass"*. CWW

Floriferous habit of 'Tapestry Rose'

'Tickled Pink'

'Tickled Pink'; ↕60cm; 6cm pale-pink single duplex spoon flowers, very pretty; mid-Sep–Oct; makes a domed bushy plant. CWW
Introduced by Home Meadow Nursery in 1994.

'Tickled Pink' flower spray

'Topsy'; RHS AGM 2012; ↕80cm; 5.5 cm single burnt chestnut-red-orange duplex flowers; mid-Sep–Oct; a self-supporting plant with greyish foliage that sets off the flowers which flower for a long time.
Bred by Mr Samuel Denis O'Brien Baker of Home Meadow Nursery in 1995 and named for his wife's school nickname.

'Topsy'

'Uri'

'Uri' flower spray

'Uri'; 2006 21d DP; ↕130cm; 6.5cm deep-pink single flowers; Oct–Nov; an upright self-supporting, clumping plant that slugs leave alone and flowers have the added bonus of a honeyed scent.

Possibly a Woolman's cultivar, the history is unknown but the name suggests the 1960s. Uri comes from the Hebrew meaning 'my flame' or 'my light'.

'Vagabond Prince' flower spray

'Vagabond Prince'

'Vagabond Prince'; 2006 21d LP; ↕110cm; 7cm wide semi-double/duplex flowers with multiple layers of a rich cyclamen-pink; Oct–Nov; upright and self-supporting growth with greyish foliage, the slugs also leave this tough plant alone.

Raised by Amos Perry and released in 1952 (he died a year later in 1953), and an original Rubellum.

'Venus 1'
early flower
form

'Venus 1' 2006; 21d LPu; ↕95cm; 5.5cm dark-pink single flowers; late-Oct–Nov; this cultivar has sweet-scented flowers that attract insects. CWW

Not to be confused with 'Venus' which has paler pink flowers, 'Venus 1' is possibly an original Bristol Nurseries (USA) plant and Korean from Alex Cummings. It can be found in Kayes' 1940s catalogue alongside all other Bristol Nurseries-listed plants. 'Kaye's glorious Koreans' referred to the Bristol chrysanthemums sold by Reginald Kaye's nursery, who sadly closed their doors in 2013.

'Vysočina'

'Vysočina'; ↕80cm; 6cm pure white double flowers forming bunches at the end of the stem; Oct–Nov; self-supporting, tough weather-proof plant. Great for cut flowers.

Sent by Prague Botanic Gardens, and introduced to the UK by collection holder Judy Barker. Vysočina is an administrative area of the Czeck Republic that incorporates Bohemia and Moldavia.

'Venus 1'
in full flower

'Vysočina' flower spray

early flower 'Wedding Day'

'Wedding Day'; 2006 21d W; ↕75-100cm; 8cm large white duplex flowers set off a green centre, opening from champagne pink buds to creamy-white petals which become fully white; mid-Oct–Nov; the large dark-green leaves redden in autumn, forming a broad loose mound; it needs a sheltered position or can be grown in a large pot. A tall plant, it makes a great cut flower as well as an excellent wedding present for gardeners. CWW

Raised by Orpington Nursery, UK in the 1950s and grown by Margery Fish who writes in chapter 15 of 'Flowers for the House' (of An All Year Garden), *'In the late autumn, there is one chrysanthemum that always finds a place in the dining-room–the fine white 'Wedding Day', with its faint scent and greenish-yellow centres.'*

'Wedding Sunshine'; 2006 21d Y; ↕70cm; 4cm single bright canary-yellow flowers; which can be somewhat floppy in habit. This is a sport of 'Wedding Day' found at Orpington Nursery, UK in the 1950s.

'Wedding Sunshine'

late flower 'Wedding Day'

'Wedding Sunshine' spray

'Wendy Tench'; 2006 21d DS; ↕40cm; 7cm plummy-red-pink duplex flowers; mid-Aug–Oct; forms a very low open bush. Raised by Elm House Nursery in the 1960s who released a Tench series, including 'Rita Tench', 'Ivy Tench' and seven other colours which have also ostensibly disappeared from cultivation, as has the nursery.

'Wendy Tench'

'White Gem'

'White Gem'; 2006 21f W; ↕60cm; 6cm single white beautiful spoon flowers; mid-Aug–Sep; an upright bush. CWW
A sport of 'Mauve Gem' it was possibly raised by Laurence Neel of Orpington Nurseries in the 1960s.
Not to be confused with the hardy annual *Chrysanthemum coronarium* 'White Gem'.

'White Gloss'

'White Gloss'; 2006 21e W; ↕90cm; 7cm pure-white almost double flowers, with a creamy centre; late Sep–Oct; forms a loose mound which can flop after rain. CWW

'White Gloss' plant habit

'White Tower'; ↕100cm; 6cm creamy-white duplex flowers; Oct–Nov; very hardy tall lax plants that benefit from support such as a small obelisk as the stems are too thin for the weight of the plants, particularly after the rain, though individual flowers are rather rain-proof.

'White Tower'

'Will's Wonderful'
flower spray

'Will's Wonderful'; RHS AGM 2012; 21d LP; ↕60cm; 3cm-sized single bicolour strawberry-red flowers, which have a paler ring surrounding a yellow centre which then fade to a straw colour leaving a red edge to the petal, open from deep-red buds; Oct–Nov; a self-supporting domed plant that is tough and slug resistant and simply delightful both for the garden and vase.

This chrysanthemum was found in Will Forster's grandmother's garden in east-central Illinois, and was re-introduced by Seneca Hill Perennials, NY, USA (now closed) under this name.

'Will's Wonderful'

'Will's Wonderful'

Further Information

The following have Plant Heritage Chrysanthemum (Hardy) Dispersed National Plant Collections®:

Mrs Judith Barker, 64 Morris Way, London Colney, AL2 1JN.
01727 822 564 judy.barker1@btopenworld.com www.gardenchrysanthemums.org.uk
Judy's NC is held in two allotments, which are locked. Access by walking past a football pitch, and stout shoes are required. Entry charge is a donation to Plant Heritage.
Best time to view is Sep—Nov, strictly by appointment, and the collection holder will meet visitors.

Dr Andrew Ward, Norwell Nurseries, Woodhouse Road, Norwell, Newark, NG23 6JX.
01636 636 337 wardha@aol.com www.norwellnurseries.co.uk
Andrew's NC is held within a one acre garden, and is open when the nursery is open.
Entry charge is by donation.
Best time to view is Sep—mid-Nov, when the nursery is open, ie 10am—5pm daily, but not Saturday or Tuesday.

Hill Close Gardens Trust, Bread and Meat Close, Warwick, CV34 6HF.
01926 493 339 centremanager@hcgt.org.uk www.hillclosegardens.com
Hill Close Gardens NC is within sixteen hedged Victorian leisure gardens, over a restored two acre site.   Entry charge to Hill Close Gardens is applicable.
Best time to view is Sep—Oct, 11am—5pm, weekdays only.

Photographic credits

The Hardy Plant Society would like to thank the following for permission to reproduce their photographs. *The HPS has been granted publishing rights for these photographs– copyright remains with the photographer.* Some of these photographers are contributors to the Hardy Plant Society's Digital Image Library www.hardy-plant.org.uk/imagelibrary

Key: page number followed by position on page, ie top left to bottom left, then top right to bottom right

Alison Cundy, RHS: 65-1
Andrew Ward, Norwell Nurseries: 14-1, 16-2, 35-2, 36-1, 36-2, 36-3, 37-1, 37-4, 38-1, 39-3, 40-3, 40-4, 41-4, 42-1,43-4, 45-5, 46-1, 46-5, 47-5, 50-4, 53-3, 53-4, 54-2, 55-4, 55-5, 56-1, 59-2, 59-4, 59-5, 61-4, 64-4, 65-4, 68-1, 68-2, 69-2, 69-3, 70-4, 72-3, 76-1, 77-4, 79-3, 79-4, 82-1, 84-1
Anna Omiotek-Tott: 77-4
Bob Brown, Cotswold Garden Flowers: 52-1, 53-1, 58-2, 70-1
Eleanor Fisher: 20-1
Gary Leaver, Hill Close Gardens: 16-1, 35-3, 36-4, 41-3, 42-3, 47-4, 51-1, 52-2, 58-5, 59-3, 60-1, 64-2, 66-2, 67-2, 69-1, 70-2, 77-3, 80-2, 80-3, 82-2, 82-4
Geoff Ashton: 45-4
HPS Conservation Scheme: 39-1, 45-3, 51-4, 52-5, 55-1, 60-6, 67-3
Irene Tibbenham: 28-1, 28-2, 29-2, 30-1, 37-5, 41-2, 48-1, 48-2, 48-3, 49-1, 49-2, 51-3, 63-2, 63-4, 64-3
John McCormack: front cover, 13-1, 16-3, 17-1, 17-3, 17-4, 18-1, 18-2, 18-3, 18-4, 18-5, 18-6, 18-7, 18-8, 19-1, 19-2, 19-3, 19-4, 19-5, 19-6, 19-7, 19-8, 23-2, 31-1, 38-2, 38-3, 40-1, 43-1, 43-3, 44-1, 44-2, 45-1, 47-1, 47-2, 47-3, 49-3, 49-4, 50-1, 50-2, 52-3, 52-4, 53-2, 54-1, 54-3, 54-4, 54-5, 55-2, 55-3, 56-3, 56-4, 56-5, 57-1, 57-2, 58-1, 59-1, 60-3, 61-3, 62-1, 62-2, 62-3, 62-4, 62-5, 62-6, 65-2, 66-4, 67-1, 69-4, 70-3, 72-1, 72-2, 73-2, 73-3, 73-4, 75-1, 75-3, 76-3, 77-5, 78-1, 78-2, 78-3, 79-2, 79-5, 80-1, 81-1, 81-3, 81-4, 83-2, 84-2, 85-1, 85-2, 85-3
John Metcalf: 41-1, 46-4, 60-4,
Judith Baker: 54-6
Judy Barker: 14-1, 15-1, 15-2, 17-2, 22-1, 23-1, 23-3, 25-1, 26-1, 30-2, 31-2, 37-2, 37-3, 35-1, 39-2, 42-2, 42-4, 43-2, 44-3, 44-4, 45-2, 46-2, 50-3, 56-2, 58-3, 58-4, 60-2, 61-1, 61-2, 64-1, 66-1, 66-3, 71-1, 71-2, 71-3, 71-4, 73-1, 75-2, 75-4, 76-2, 77-1, 77-2, 79-1, 80-4, 81-2, 82-3, 83-1, 84-3
Lawrence Smith: 63-1, 63-3
Marianne Majerus: 27-1
Martin Hughes-Jones, Sampford Shrubs: 38-4
Pat Cryer: 29-1
Peter Darrell: 9-1
Rosemary Mitchell, Hill Close Gardens: 26-2
Sophie Leguil: 38-5
Susan Rowe: 40-2, 46-3
Tricia Fraser: 51-2, 60-5
Trevor Walton: 65-3
W. Atlee Burpee Company: 74-1, 74-2